A Cheap and Cheeky Guide to Birdwatching

Welcome to birdwatching, which, from now on, I will refer to as 'birding'. It saves a syllable. Also it sounds a bit cooler – well, inasmuch as birding can be cool.

This is a guide to getting started in a huge, beautiful, and at times daunting hobby.

I've basically been birding since I could walk, and have picked up a thing or two along the way. I've also got a lot wrong, and by learning from my mistakes, this little book should save you some of the expense, frustration, discomfort and embarrassment I have experienced over the years.

I don't like wasting words, so let's get started.

Why bird?

If you've started reading this mini-tome, then you surely have your own reasons for getting into birding. There are probably as many reasons for birding as there are birders. But just in case you're on the fence, let me convince you.

It's a great way to connect with nature – If you love the outdoors, then birding is the perfect way to enhance that experience. As you get to grips with the cycles of the birding year, you gain a deeper appreciation of the changing seasons, either by recognising new arrivals in the spring and autumn, or by observing the changing behaviour of the birds as the months roll by.

And more than that, by looking at one part of nature in detail, you begin to experience the connectedness of everything – you'll notice that this particular bird is catching caterpillars to feed its babies, and that those caterpillars were laid by this particular butterfly, which only lays eggs on this one particular plant, which only grows in this particular type of soil. There's something satisfying about making these connections, and it makes you feel really small and ignorant in the face of such complex webs of interconnectivity - in a good way, that is!

Birds are fascinating – And beautiful (except swans, those overblown, overrated, preening divas). Did you know that the tiny Goldcrest (the anti-swan), despite weighing as much as a 5p coin, flies here across the North Sea from Scandinavia? Or that the Swift, other than when in the nest for a few short weeks of the year, never lands? Or that a woodpecker's tongue is so long that it wraps around its brain inside its skull and acts as a cushion when it's whacking its head against a tree? I could go on.

GOLDCREST

It's good for you – It gets you out of the house, and often involves plenty of walking, so unless you are doing it in a freezing gale, it's good for your physical health. Also, all those peaceful early mornings when you are absorbed in the meditative activity of simply searching and listening are surely beneficial – you are one hundred percent in the moment and not worrying about checking your emails. So it's good for your mental health, too – though you probably wouldn't suspect that given some of the birders you'll meet.

It will satiate desires for list making – Who doesn't like being able to tick things off a list? Even better if you're ticking off something really difficult that took years to achieve, right? Of course, you could get into train spotting, but you *know* where they're going to be and when (within the limits of the British Rail system), so I don't really see the challenge. Birds, mysterious little devils that they are, can turn up anywhere, or decide not to turn up at all, adding a real element of excitement and unpredictability to any outing.

It's something to do, innit? – As far as hobbies go, you could do worse. It isn't expensive (unless you want it to be), it gets you out the house, there is minimal risk of injury or death, and people will find you cool and interesting. Okay, that last one was a fib, but I stand by the others.

Getting kitted out

Unlike, say, mountain climbing, birding keeps the kit to a minimum, but there are still a lot of misconceptions and pitfalls to avoid when buying your two or three essential items.

Binoculars - The quintessential (and essential) birdwatching tool. As with anything where different companies are trying to sell you their product, there is a lot of confusion and disinformation about which 'bins' to buy. Let me make it simple.

Zoom and Field. When browsing binoculars, there are two numbers that appear and look something like this 10x42. The first number is how many times 'zoom' they provide you with. The second is how large an area you see when looking through them. So, the bigger the better, right? Wrong!

Don't get suckered into buying a pair of 20x zoom binoculars. It sounds great, but in reality, unless you have the steady hands of a bomb-disposal expert, 20x is just too much. You'll be wobbling all over the place and unable to spot anything.

10x is the maximum you will need, and 8x is perfectly fine.

As for the second number, well, bigger *is* better here. Just bear in mind that a big field of view means big clunky binoculars that you will be lugging around and lifting. Somewhere in the 32 or 42 range should be perfect.

Waterproof? Yes. Even if you don't intend on going out in the rain, waterproof binoculars are a good idea. If not, they have an annoying habit of steaming up rendering them useless. Also, if you're birding in Britain, you will, at some point, regardless of your intentions, be birding in the rain.

Glass type. Things get a little tricky here, but for beginners' purposes, it's not too important. If you can afford binoculars with ED (extra low dispersion) glass, then get them. They basically produce a brighter, sharper image. Some lenses have coloured coatings on them and these have their advantages and disadvantages - until things start to get serious, you won't need to worry about this at all.

Brand. The top brands of binoculars without a doubt are Leica and Swarowski – but these are insanely expensive. I'm talking upwards of a thousand pounds. And although these are obviously brilliant optics with amazing customer service, you can get a perfectly serviceable pair of bins for a fraction of the price. Viking, Opticron and Nikon, in my opinion, seem to inhabit the top-end of the affordable spectrum. If this is still too expensive, then just spend as much as you can on what you can. Just as long as they're the right zoom and are waterproof, you'll be fine.

ID guide - An identification guide is the next essential. There are loads to choose from, but I'll keep it simple. Get the *Collins Bird Guide* (ISBN 9780007268146). It's the best one.

What? You want justification? Well, the drawings are perfect (and better than photos for ID purposes), it has just the right level of detail and concision, it has all the birds you could possibly see in the UK in it, the layout is ideal, and it ain't too heavy.

Scope and tripod - No need to dive in here straight away, but at some point, you will consider buying a telescope. They are particularly useful in bird hides or when sea watching, as both involve sitting still for ages and looking at specks in the distance. But your binoculars will always be your primary weapon – you use the big field of view and maneuverability to find your target, and only then use the scope for a closer snoop if necessary. With this in mind, as a beginner, you will still see really good birds through a really bad scope.

Telescopes are expensive, so if you're desperate for one, then consider getting one second hand. You are looking for a birding scope or 'spotting scope', as opposed to an astronomical scope.

When deciding, apply pretty much the same rules for scopes as for bins. Make sure it's waterproof, has ED glass if you can afford it, and comes from a reputable company. As for zoom, again, no need to go crazy! Some scopes will offer up to 70x zoom, or even adjustable zoom. In my experience, all this means is you end up

fiddling around and zooming in and out on a Godwit's eye for ages. Too much faff. Even a modest zoom like 32x will seem like an amazing improvement on your 10x binoculars and is perfectly good.
Remember, that the scope will also have a bigger lens than your bins, so will provide a sharp, clear, bright image, which also doesn't wobble because....

You bought a tripod to go with it! At high zooms, images will wobble uncontrollably unless using a sturdy tripod. Make sure that you buy one which has long enough legs to pcek out of the hide and doesn't buckle under the weight of your scope.

The bottom line with optics is get some good binoculars. Whatever you have left you can use to buy a scope.

Note book and pencil - A bit old-school perhaps, but you can't beat a notebook for scribbling down what you've seen and looking back on it later. You might even have a go at doing a sketch. I suppose you could keep notes on your phone, nowadays, but there's always the chance you'll run out of batteries or drop it in a puddle. Also, it's nice to look back through your old notebooks – it's amazing how they jog the memory and take you back to the exact moment you saw that Goshawk.

Smartphone – An increasingly important piece of kit for the modern birder as it's great to be able to get some updates on the move. Let's say you've made a trip to a particular hide to see a bird that's been there all week – it's incredibly reassuring to be able to look at *Twitter* and see that it's still there. Or maybe it's flown down the road and you can make a quick detour rather than sitting expectantly in an empty hide. You can return the favour, too. If you do see something really special, you'll want to get the news out so others can enjoy it (and so that someone else can see it and prove you haven't gone mad). Again, invaluable. Also, you can keep track of the weather, tides, wind direction, maps, public transport etc. You might even be able to get a shaky photo on a modern phone that will help with identification or record keeping.

Some good walking boots and waterproofs - Will be good friends in the inevitably inclement weather, but there is literally no need to get a load of camo gear like you will see some chumps wearing. The bird has either seen you or it hasn't, and it either cares or it doesn't – I don't imagine that wearing green makes any realistic difference.

And that's it!

Using Binoculars

Everyone assumes you will know how to do this, but I'm about to give you a few handy tips which will save you a lot of bother.

Start with your eyes - Look at the bird first, then bring your binoculars up to your eyes. There's nothing more frustrating than someone who starts with their binoculars to their face, then starts rotating about going "Where is it? I can't see it!"

Think about it. You are already looking at the bird – don't let it out of your sight! Keep a fixed gaze on it, then slowly draw the binoculars into the space between you and the bird – hey presto! You are now looking directly at it through your bins.

Keep the strap short - Binoculars on a long strap will not only be miles away from your face when you need them, but will swing about and bounce off your beer belly – very uncomfortable.

Focus - Use the little wheel on top to alter the focus. Keep going beyond the sharpest image into fuzziness and then back again to find the absolute optimum clarity. What not everyone knows, is that most binoculars have another little focus knob on one eyepiece. This is for people with one eye better than the other. If this is you, get the main focus right for one eye, then close that eye and fiddle with the secret focus knob until that one's clear, too.

Lose the lens caps - They are annoying and time consuming. When you aren't using your bins you'll have them in their case anyway. There certainly isn't time 'in the field' to be farting around removing and applying little rubber cups to your optics.

Give them a wipe every now and then - Lenses can get dusty, mucky or salt-sprayed over time (especially if you lost the lens caps like I suggested), so use a really soft glasses cloth to give them a brush-up every now and then. No need to stick them under the tap or anything – that'll probably do more harm than good. Also, there is no need to get obsessive about this. You'd be surprised how clearly you can see through a slightly grubby lens. If you are having trouble seeing something clearly, it's more likely that something is wrong with your bins than that they are dirty.

First Steps

So, where to start with your lovely new binoculars? Taking the first steps into a huge, complex hobby can be daunting, but, luckily, birding is just looking at birds, and anyone can do that, right?

SONGTHRUSH

Well, actually it is a little more complicated than that. After all, what is the goal when we're birding? I think it boils down to one thing - identification. Some birders will tell you that they are just there to observe the majesty and behaviour of the birds and aren't interested in noting the species... but they aren't being completely honest with you. Even the most list-averse birder will know their Song Thrush from their Mistle Thrush, and just watch them if a Blue Rock Thrush turns up – not so disinterested in identification now are they?

Whether you're actively keeping a list (much more on these later) or not, the heart of birding is still identification, and this is what you'll want to be able to do. That's not to say that identifying birds is all you are doing – of course you will want to watch them and wonder at them – but you still want to be able to describe what you're seeing.

How then, do you get started with identification? The answer is to start easy and build up. You can probably identify a few species already. The trick is to familiarise yourself with common species, so that when something you don't recognise appears, you register it as something different – you can then look it up, and you've expanded your identification repertoire by one.

Start with some incidental birding. Look at the world like a birder when you're going about your everyday life. That bird hopping along the hedgerow – was that a Dunnock or a Wren? A handful of crows flying overhead – were they Crows or Rooks? That colourful little bird coming to the feeder – was that a Great Tit or a Blue Tit?

Of course, this all gets complicated pretty quickly, as birds are not only often sexually dimorphous (a fancy way of saying males and females are different colours), but might even change their feathers, and thus their colours, throughout the year. Juvenile birds, in particular, can look very nondescript and scruffy. Because of this, you will soon realise that the size, shape and movement of the bird are the most reliable quick indicators of what you're looking at rather than the colour of its beak, for instance. Anyway, let's not get ahead of ourselves – there's a whole chapter on identification later.

If you're not sure what something is, you'll want to look it up in your *Collins Guide*. Birds are arranged into family groups with birds of similar size and shape. Flip through until you're in the right section then peruse more thoroughly to look at your candidates. Ignore the rare birds with *** symbols next to them – it wasn't one of them, as much as you might want to believe it. Don't be afraid to read the text on the species, too, as there is often some real giveaway about behaviour in there. For example it might say that the bird likes to hop about low in hedgerows, or has a habit of pumping its tail up and down – Aha! Exactly what you just witnessed!

Now you've made a start, you'll want to get out to somewhere interesting. Check online for local reserves, or visit your county bird news website (yes, you've probably got one) to find where the other birders go. Obviously, there can be a vast difference in the type and quality of nature reserves, so I can't guarantee any success here, but the chances are you'll see something new, especially if the habitat is something different and it's the right time of year. Reserves will usually have information boards telling you what sorts of things you can see – really useful to the novice birder. They will also be home to other birders who can help you out – some of these might even be knowledgeable and approachable!

With that in mind, is there any birding etiquette you should know about? If there is, then you should be reassured to know that most birders don't seem to know it! I think this boils down to one simple rule – the birds' welfare is paramount. Basically, don't try and get too close and don't make an almighty racket - this will cause the birds discomfort, scare them off, and make any other birders in the vicinity very angry with you.

Well done. You've dipped your toe into the big, wide world of birding. If you want to bundle around and make your own mistakes, then you can stop reading here. However, if you want to get good, and get the most out of it quickly, we're about to get into all the interesting stuff.

When and Where

The birder's year

As I already alluded to in the introduction, birding really helps you get in synch with the changing seasons and the rhythms of nature. Each season brings its own excitements and challenges, and knowing what to expect and where to be at the different times of year is one of the things that separates a bumbling birdwatcher from a dynamic and successful birder.

January and February - At this time of year, things tend to be pretty settled and quiet. Hardly any birds are singing, all the insect-eating summer birds are in sunnier climes, and our resident birds are predictably going about their business – eating and sleeping. January and February rarely throw up any surprises. But there are still some good things to try...

Estuaries and lakes, for example. All of our summer birds have flown south for the winter, but there are places north of us, for whom we are the south. Notably, this applies to wading birds, and wildfowl who spend the winter in Britain before travelling back to Scandinavia and Siberia. These birds love water and mud (in which they feed), so this is a super time to get down to river estuaries or mud-fringed lakes to see what's happening. Sometimes, there are rare and interesting ducks and waders about, but more often this is great just for the spectacle and variety on show. Ducks and geese are colourful and flamboyant and easy to watch as they waddle or swim about making a huge racket. Waders are a bit trickier, mostly being variations on a long billed, long-legged, brownish theme, but are spectacular when swooping about in large numbers or noisily jostling over worms.

Extreme weather can also liven up a birder's winter. Blizzards and unusually severe weather will shake things up in the birding world. In these conditions, birds desperate for food will flee areas of frozen ground and feed wherever they can, meaning birds like Lapwings or Woodcock might turn up in your suburban garden. If winter gets really bad in Scandinavia or Siberia (that is, even worse than normal), we might get an influx of unusual visitors like Waxwings.

And don't forget your birdfeeders! Small garden birds need help through the winter, so you'll find that this is the best time of year for seeing activity in your garden if you're lucky enough to have one. There's a delightful array of colourful little finches, and tits (as well as the less colourful, but equally delightful, thrushes and sparrows) who'll come and liven up your garden if you put out food for them.

March and April - Can you feel that? That's the electricity of expectation! With the first signs of spring, comes just about the most exciting time of year to be birding.

Why? Migration. This is the time of year when things begin to move. This not only means that new birds are arriving from further south, but our wintering wildfowl and waders are beginning to move north. So, as well as there being lots of new things to see, in all this chaos, birds turn up in all sorts of unexpected places. It's brilliant.

Probably the best places to go at this time of year are to headlands, islands, or the coast, especially when the wind and weather conditions are right. The majority of little birds migrate overnight, and seem to prefer clear nights when the wind is behind them to make their journey easier. At their first sight of land, these little birds will want to stop and refuel. If bad weather hits just before dawn, this effect can be even more extreme, with fog, rain or strong winds literally forcing birds out of the sky onto the first available piece of land. So, imagine a March morning where the wind has been flowing up from the continent on a clear night, with the weather suddenly turning just before sunrise, with you ready on a headland full of bushes at the crack of dawn – you might just be lucky enough to experience a 'fall', where birds are everywhere! Surely one of the best moments a birder can hope for. What makes these 'falls' even more exciting is how difficult they are to predict.

It's not just headlands, either. Anywhere where there are 'passageways' into the country can be great places to be in spring. This could be a park or a wood or a strip of farmland where there is an uninterrupted passageway of nature from the coast to the areas inland where the birds breed. Lakes, reservoirs and gravel pits provide refueling spots for water birds, so these become a great place to observe at this time of year, as well.

And to make matters even more exciting, not only are you going to get loads of common and beautiful migrants arriving in stages through the month, you also encounter the possibility of something really unusual turning up. Birds who would usually use spring to move from Africa to Southern Europe might 'overshoot' in their migration and turn up in Britain. Be prepared for anything!

It's also really satisfying to see the birds arriving on schedule. Sand Martins first, then Wheatears, then Willow Warblers and House Martins. Swallows a little later. Then into April, with Reed Warblers, Cuckoos, and Pied Flycatchers. Spotted Flycatchers later still. You might not see a Swift or a Nightjar until...

May and June - Into May, and migration continues. But some birds have been here a little while and are already staking out territory and building nests. Because of this, May is a good time to go to places where birds breed – woodland, farmland and moorland. Sometimes a late spring morning can be overwhelmingly cacophonous, with the dawn chorus in full splendour.

As well as being noisy, the birds are easy to see at this time of year, as they busily go about their business of displaying to mates, protecting their territory and gathering materials for their nests.

As in the other spring months, you are really spoilt for choice, here. Go where you want and you'll likely find something to excite you. May is particularly notorious for rarities if that's your thing.

Then things begin to quieten down a little in June, as the birds all have their nests in place and get into the business of raising their young. Because of this, it can be a really good time of year to go and look for nesting seabirds – if there are cliffs near you, then there is a good chance that there will be nesting colonies of auks, Fulmars and Kittiwakes, which make a wonderful noisy spectacle.

KITTIWAKE

And then...

July and August - Ugh. Nothing. The nadir of the birding year. Which is doubly annoying as it's the best time to get out of doors. So it goes.

Why does it suddenly get so dead? Basically, the birds have mated, raised their young and have nothing to do until it's time to migrate back to warmer climes. Then like many a married man in the middle of his life, they let themselves go a bit. They will need to grow new feathers for the big migration, so they go into moult and become indistinct, scruffy and occasionally flightless creatures for a few weeks. As such, they keep a low profile. And the young keep a low profile, too, no longer squeaking or squawking to be fed, but trying to skulk about and avoid being eaten by predators. Nowhere is this better illustrated than the woods – go to the same place that was alive with the dawn chorus in May, and you will find it spookily quiet.

Many birders manage to keep their obsession alive in these months by getting into lepidoptery (Butterflies and Moths) or studying odontera (Dragonflies), but it's not quite the same.

There is, though, one place where the birding is quite exciting in these otherwise desert months – would you like to hear about it? Whisper it – sea watching. Sea watching seems like a weird cult subsection of birding where you wait for summer storms, then sit in the most exposed places possible to spot distant lost seabirds through a scope. We'll talk more about this later.

September and October - And we're back in business! September and October are just as good, if not better than spring, as all the migration kicks off again!

This time, the islands and headlands are places for birds to stop and have one last feed-up before crossing the sea back to the continent. They won't stick around for long, and if the weather is particularly fine, they'll shoot straight overhead, so your best bets are grey and drizzly mornings.

The winter birds start returning, so as well as catching the departing passerines (perchy birds), there are new and exciting water birds appearing left, right and centre.

Sea watching, too, if it's your kind of thing continues to be good in these months.

And, again, lost rarities start turning up all over the place.

November and December - Migration and its associated excitement continues into early November, before things begin to return to Januaryesque drudgery.

A nice addition to the returning water birds, is the arrival of winter thrushes – Redwings and Fieldfares, particularly, who can arrive from the continent in huge flocks ready to strip every berry off every bush for miles around. Listen out at night for Redwings migrating overhead with a thin, high pitched 'seep'! One of the most evocative sounds of the birding year for me.

Time of day

On a more 'micro' level, does it matter what time of day you go birding? Well, yes, usually!

The early birder catches the bird that catches the worm. Birds are at their most active first thing in the morning when they wake up hungry and need to get some caterpillars in their gut before a long day of flapping about. Also, at the right time of year, early morning is when the dawn chorus is at its crescendo, so that makes for a great experience, too.

Sadly, this means getting up early, but it's worth it! Try and head out while it's still dark, timing your arrival at your destination with first light. There is, however, such a thing as being too early, especially on a cold day – many birds wake up with the insects they feed on, so you might be waiting for the first vestiges of warmth before any activity occurs.

Even sea birds seem to be most active at this time. If you decide to indulge in a spot of sea watching, it is important to get there for first light when the first wave of lost seabirds realize they are in the wrong place and start bombing it back to the open ocean.

Also, the morning air creates thermals as the land heats up, and this is the ideal time for seeing birds of prey, who use these towers of hot air to soar up and view their hunting grounds below.

The middle of the day, though, coincides with a weird slump in bird activity. There are still birds around, but they seem to enjoy midday for a siesta, so use this time to have your lunch and a perhaps little snooze of your own.

Things pick up again towards the evening, when birds try and get one last feed before bed. Also, there is a lot of movement here as birds find their way to roosts – a safe place for the night. Sometimes, early evenings can be quite spectacular times to see birds congregate in vast flocks. You can also get a kind of evening chorus – just think of that evocative sound of Blackbirds whistling lazily into a summer's evening.

Dusk, too brings a particular magic, when Owls are waking up to enjoy a night of mischief. Get out and see them at dusk, as it will be too dark to see them once the sun fully sets.

Habitats

So, now you aren't going to embarrass yourself by looking for warblers in December or ducks in August, you can start thinking about where you should be heading. The magic of evolution is the way in which species adapt to fill all kinds of interesting niches. Certain birds require very specific habitats and food sources, so if there's a species you really want to see, then you will improve your chances by doing your research and heading to the right place.

Some birds are ubiquitous, some are even gregarious, but many are fussy little devils and like conditions just right. Having a sound knowledge of the places that birds inhabit will help you get the best out of your early birding journeys and ensure you find what you're looking for.

Of course, where you are in the country is important, too, and you will soon learn the idiosyncrasies and weaknesses of your own patch. For starters, though, let me just discuss the different habitats and their merits.

Forest - The woods are just about the worst place to begin birding. There are leaves in the way, for a start. And in the middle of summer, especially, you won't see a thing. Also, woodland species in this country tend to be an all-year-round affair so you won't find many exciting new birds each time you visit.

That said, there are some really great birds to be found in woodland that are hard to find anywhere else - woodpeckers, Nuthatches and Treecreepers all year round, and certain warblers and flycatchers in the summer.

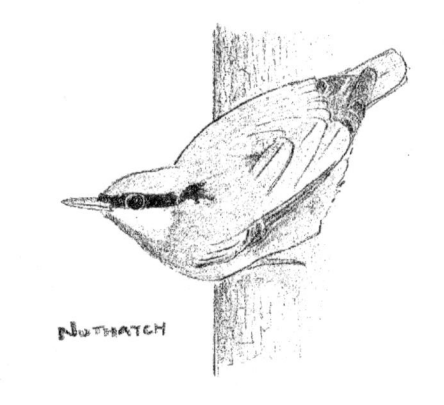

NUTHATCH

The type of forest or woodland you are visiting can make a big difference - a conifer plantation might be a bit of a wildlife desert, whereas a mixed deciduous woodland, at the right time of year, can be bursting with life. That said, birds always find a niche, and Spruce plantations will be just about the only place you'll see a Crossbill.

The best time to go birding in the woods is spring. If you aim for early spring, the leaves won't be fully out yet, allowing you to actually see the birds, while a visit in mid to late spring will give you chance to find those migrants as they sing and build nests. Nowhere is learning bird song and calls more important than when woodland birding. More on that later!

Coast - Coastal sites are usually the best places for birding. Partly for the chance of seeing migration in action, but also because you are essentially straddling two habitats – the sea and the land.

Cliffs and headlands are (as discussed earlier) some of the best places to bird, so if you're lucky enough to live near this habitat, consider making it your regular stomping ground.

Areas of scrub and trees on top of headlands are great places to look for migrants in spring and autumn, and you can also look for birds flying overhead, though this can be quite a tricky skill to develop, identifying the little dots as they whizz over at great height! The cliffs themselves, will be home to some interesting sights, too. Seabirds like Shags, Kittiwakes, Fulmars and auks nest on cliff ledges, and though you're unlikely to find something 'rare' here, it can be quite a noisy and enjoyable spectacle when seabirds are raising their young, swooping up onto the perilous ledges to feed them.

Beaches and spits can also make great birding sites at the right time of year – especially if there is some cover for migrating birds. Many a rarity has been found hopping about on a beach. Summer is a good time to watch terns fishing off the sandy shore, and winter might bring divers and scoters close to shore. The only problem here is finding beach habitats that aren't full of holiday makers and dog walkers scaring your birds away!

To get the best out of coastal birding, you also want to have an eye on the weather and the tide. Strong winds on a clifftop mean that you aren't going to see many little birds as they seek shelter somewhere safe, but those same storms might be good for sea watching if shearwaters, skuas and other strange seabirds are pushed in towards the land. As for the tide, a receding tide will create shallow traps for fish and therefore attract the birds that prey on them, and low tide exposes rock pools which might attract egrets, herons or even Kingfishers.

Estuaries - Another place where knowing the tide times is important. Estuaries are among some of the best places for birding, as they attract waders and wildfowl which feed in the mud. Where rivers meet the sea, there is a wonderful mixture of fresh and saltwater habitat encouraging life to bloom.

As we've already established, estuaries are best for winter birding, but getting the tide time right is paramount. If the tide is right out, then all the birds will be very distant, feeding out on the mudflats. If the tide is at its highest, then there might be no mud at all, causing the waders to fly off and go to sleep somewhere. A wise birder will time their arrival at an estuary either with the tide falling, so that they can watch the birds arrive to feed as the water recedes, or when the tide is rising, allowing them to watch the birds get 'pushed' closer and closer to their vantage point as they try and get a few last mouthfuls of lugworm before nap time.

Rivers and lakes - Fresh water habitats provide some of the most specific places for birding in this country. The flow of a river, and even the geology, will have a huge effect on what birds you can see there.

DIPPER

The Dipper, for instance – an adorable and characterful bird reminiscent of a Christmas pudding – only likes stony fast-flowing streams and rivers, while a Kingfisher prefers slower-moving clear waters. Sand Martins nest specifically by burrowing into sandy banks on the side of rivers, so will only occur in places where this type of soil is found.

Often, of course, a river will coincide with woodland, farmland or some other habitat, so a magnifying synergy occurs. As anyone who's been attacked by midges will attest, fresh water is a boon for insects, and as many bird species are largely insectivorous, they are super places for birds to feed and raise their young.

Lakes are different again. And in parts of the country where large areas of standing water are rare, a lake can be a beacon for migrating water birds. Sometimes a really lost seabird can turn up on a lake, causing some excitement for local birders, though these events are tinged with sadness, as the bird usually dies away from its salty home.

Wetland - By which I mean reed beds and swamps. These can be among the most exciting places to bird, but also the most frustrating. There is a similarity with forest birding in that you can often hear the birds, but have to be insanely patient to see them. Birds like Cetti's Warblers, Bitterns and Water Rails have a particularly irritating habit of being extremely noisy and also extremely shy – entirely reticent to leave their little world of reed stems.

CETTI'S WARBLER

But, if you have the patience, this habitat contains some of Britain's most charismatic species. In summer, singing Reed and Sedge Warblers are a joy, and

Hobbies use these habitats as hunting grounds for their dragonfly prey.

The winter, too, holds its own charm in these places. Wildfowl love reedy wetlands, and birds of prey like Marsh Harriers make the most of the duck paté. Perhaps best of all, Starlings like to roost in reed beds, so if you want to see a spectacular murmuration, a winter's evening in your local wetlands is likely to be your best bet.

Farmland - Sadly, this is probably the most changed and damaged habitat in this country. Old (and admittedly pretty inefficient) farming techniques used to support really interesting ecosystems. Now, the large swathes of industrial farmland are effectively devoid of wildlife. Not just because of the loss of hedgerows, but because of the use of pesticides which have decimated the insect population on which the birds feed.

That said, in places where there are hedgerows and arable farming, especially if traditional techniques are maintained, there can be some really special birds to be seen here. In fact, I would go as far as to say that searching for farmland birds is the most 'British' feeling birding experience you can have – as if you're living in some Victorian poem.

In spring and summer, hedgerows are important breeding places for buntings and other small birds, and nothing reminds me more stirringly of my childhood in rural Britain as the sound of a Yellowhammer singing from a sunny telephone wire. Other sounds, though, like the purring of a Turtle Dove or the distinctive croak of a Corn Crake are increasingly rare.

In winter, if farms leave the 'stubble' in their fields, flocks of finches and buntings come to feed in the furrows. Sorting through these little birds with binoculars can be eye-watering, but there is always the chance of something interesting, maybe a Brambling or a Woodlark mixed in with commoner species.

Although arable farming is generally more favourable to bird life, there are a few birds who associate with farm animals, too. Swallows and martins feast on the flies that gather around livestock, and, as such, can often be seen swooping low over cattle.

Yellow Wagtails, too, take advantage of the insects attracted to cows and can be seen scampering among their hooves in the summer months. And Cattle Egrets are called that for a reason!

Moors, heaths and mountains - Can, on first sight, be desolate and birdless, but as with all niche habitats, provide places for a few specialist species.

The problem with a lot of moorland in this country is that it is over-managed, or else completely mismanaged. Sadly, this means that where there could be scrub and forest, there is instead an over-grazed desert. This does suit a few birds – Skylarks, Wheatears and Meadow Pipits in summer, and can provide important breeding grounds for waders, but is a very poor habitat for the majority of species. As a result, the best places are either heaths specifically managed as wildlife reserves, or places where moorland borders other, more diverse habitats like forests or rivers.

For example, the wonderful and mysterious Nightjar can be found nesting on heaths, but likes to be near areas of forest, too. Similarly, Whitethroats,

Grasshopper Warblers and even Dartford Warblers love low scrubby heath of the sort that can be found on moorland fringes where the vegetation has been allowed to develop.

Moors and mountains also have the benefit of being attractive to all sorts of birds of prey – Buzzards, Merlins, Red Kites, Hen Harriers, even Golden Eagles if you are in Scotland. Beware, though, these keen-eyed birds will see you long before you've seen them, and are (with good reason) very wary of humans – you'll need to get good at identifying distant silhouettes as they disappear over a ridge.

Urban areas - Finally, let's not forget the towns and cities. Obviously, these aren't going to be the best birding sites, and you'll feel a bit creepy wandering around with binoculars, but there are more than just Pigeons to be seen if you activate 'birding mode' in the city.

Parks, obviously, provide little refuges for nature, and often have good numbers of the commoner species. As little oases in urban landscapes, they can sometimes turn up a migrating rarity, too. In many areas of the country, incongruous Ring-Necked Parakeets are making parks their unlikely homes – they are striking and engaging birds, even if their long-term impact is unknown.

Outside of the parks, look out for Peregrines – surely, one of our most iconic birds – who like to nest on old churches or other tall buildings. Their noisy cry as they swoop in to feed their young will often give them away!

Another thing to look out for in town is the local Pied Wagtail roost. 'P-Wags' are very common, and although they spend the day either alone or in small groups, like to reconvene in the evening and sleep huddled up in a particular tree or on a particular roof. Once you have located one of these sites it can be quite amazing to see how many of these noisy little charmers turn up. If you pass their favourite tree late at night, look up – it will look like it is full of fluffy white Christmas decorations!

Weather

As well as going to the right place at the right time, the successful birder keeps an eye on the weather.

Little birds seem to disappear completely in strong winds and rain, so going to the woods in a storm will be as pointless as it is foolish. On the other hand, seabirds adore storms, and birds like waders and wildfowl are largely ambivalent towards extreme weather of this kind.

Really extreme weather, such as snow and blizzards can have interesting (if devastating effects) on bird life. And it's worth going for an explore in the snow to see what's been displaced by frozen ground or has desperately fled to the refuge of gardens and bird feeders.

What about the opposite? Well, blazing calm heat (rare enough in this country for sure), seems to be pretty counterproductive, too. Just like ourselves, birds don't want to get overheated or dehydrated, and tend to indulge in a bit of a siesta in hot weather. Also, this type of weather is associated with the dead birding months of July and August. Hot weather is good for creating thermals, though, which can make it good raptor spotting weather – Red Kites and the like may take advantage of dry, hot days to 'disperse' - soar about and look for a new place to live.

Really, the best weather for birding is when it's pretty still. A bit of drizzle or a bit of sun won't make much difference either way, but the wind is an important factor. If it is migration time, then the wind direction can become really important, too. Use your logic – If you are on the east coast in autumn, then birds are going to drift over the North Sea on a westerly wind, if you are in the West Country in spring, then a northerly will help birds across the channel. Bear in mind, though, that birds love to confound your expectations and might just struggle into a head wind to annoy you.

As mentioned before, mist is counter-intuitively one of the best weather conditions for birders. Sure, your view is limited, but so is the birds'. Nothing forces

little migrating birds down onto your patch
like a fog bank.

Bird Hides

At some point, you will end up in a bird hide. Maybe it's just because of some childhood nostalgia, but I love being in a hide: the smell of the mouldering wood, the squeak of the hinges on those silly little windows, the cold air wafting in. Personally, I like nothing better than having a hide to myself where I can munch on a packed breakfast and sip a flask of tea while scanning to and fro with my scope.

They can be great places for watching birds. But not all bird hides are created equal – you will soon learn which are well placed and which are next to worthless. Make sure you are visiting at the right time of year, and in the right weather, and at the right time of day, and, perhaps, at the right tide time, too. Hides on estuaries, marshes and lakes will probably be best visited with a scope, but it's not a necessity.

And of course, they are a good place to meet other birders. Much as I like a hide to myself, more observers means more chance of spotting that rarity as it scoots past or disappears into a flock of Dunlin. Some patch-loyal birders may have a real dedication to a certain hide and will be able to tell you just where to look for different species, or exactly what time the terns will turn up.

Is there some hide etiquette you should know? Some birders will insist on being very quiet in a hide, but in reality, it isn't that important – I always assume the birds know you're there anyway, or else they are too far away to care. Of course, you don't want to be bellowing and guffawing, nor do you want your Metallica ringtone to suddenly shatter the silence, but anyone insisting on a hushed reverie in a hide is being overly precious. Try and close the door quietly behind you as not to give anyone a heart-attack.

Don't be shy about opening windows (maybe ask if people want them left open when you leave), or seeing if someone will shuffle up on a bench if there isn't much room. If you enter a hide and someone is already there, summon the courage to ask what they've seen – you'll feel really awkward if you don't and then see something interesting, and have to then ask them if they've seen it.

Which leads us neatly on to our next topic…

Birders

Types of Birder

What sort of birder are you going to be, then?

As mentioned earlier, people bird for different reasons, and, as such, you are likely to meet a whole range of 'characters' out on your birding adventures. Just remember that birding does tend to attract the odder members of society, so don't expect many balanced and normal humans. Instead they tend to gravitate towards two extremes - delightful, helpful, and warm, or else grumpy, patronising and incommunicative.

Look out for snobbery. I once saw a chap in a hide getting incredibly excited about seeing a Wheatear "It's my new favourite bird!" he cried, as the arranged birders looked to one another with smirks. I can see their point – they've seen thousands of Wheatears, and it's a sad fact that the more you look at something the less interesting it becomes. But at the same time, a Wheatear is a really beautiful bird – kind of noble and delicate in its pastel tones and upright bearing, and that bloke who'd never seen one before was entirely in his rights to be delighted.

Worse, perhaps, is a kind of inverted snobbery. Many a time I've asked a birder if they've "Seen anything interesting about?" and they have audibly scoffed - everything is interesting to them! Oh, so pure, so balanced is their pursuit of their hobby that a Robin is of equal value to them as a Bluethroat. I can understand this to a degree – if you stop worrying about lists and new experiences for a minute, you can appreciate the beautiful song of a Robin or the striking colours of a Magpie, but it is disingenuous to suggest that these daily occurrences are equally interesting as a beautiful lost little Siberian passerine in all its mysterious splendour.

Give snobs and inverse snobs short shrift and get on with your day.

What follows is an attempt to 'categorise' birders. Of course, real people are likely to be a mixture of these categories, and you will find the whole spectrum of human nature across them.

Birdwatcher - It is probably safe to say that anyone calling themselves a birdwatcher isn't really that into it. As such, it is a term that applies to the passive enjoyment of birds in your own garden, and maybe popping into a bird hide if you pass one on a walk.

Birdwatchers don't find rare birds, don't carry scopes, and like to ask birders what they are looking at.

Birder - One who actively seeks out birds to identify and enjoy. A birder will be setting off on little adventures with the specific intention of finding birds. This might involve getting up early, getting rained on, or getting a numb bum from patiently sitting in a hide for hours on end - but it is the intention and dedication that separates them from a birdwatcher.

Birders are likely to keep a list, and probably have a little notebook with them. They have a hankering for birds they haven't seen before, or haven't seen that year. When they encounter a new bird, they study it and observe it, adding to their ever-growing 'schema' of species – "Oh, I see, it is a lot like the Common Redshank, but the eye-stripe is quite distinctive, and look how it moves a little differently..." This allows the birder to be constantly improving their skills and getting better at quickly identifying a Spotted Redshank next time they encounter one.

But they are not necessarily obsessive...

Twitcher - Twitchers are the extreme end of birding. Twitchers are what happens when the list becomes the aim rather than the result of a birding trip.

I would define a twitcher as one who travels great distances at the drop of a hat to add to their list. Or one of their lists anyway! Twitchers might not only keep a life list, UK list, year list, but maybe a list for each county! Many will have a Scilly list or a Fair Isle list, as these are the absolute Mecca of rarity finding in the UK in spring and autumn.

Twitchers have a bit of a bad rep. Sometimes this is well-earned - for instance, when they turn up en-mass and trample their way over a local reserve, or when they use bird call recordings on their phones to lure out an exhausted rarity from a bush. They also have a reputation for not really 'appreciating' the birds they tick off their lists. Indeed, I have seen twitchers turn up to a site, raise their bins to a bird for a second, scribble in their notebook and leave. A bit of a shame, maybe.

But, in the main, Twitchers are very good birders. They have to be to make sure they are ticking the right bird – when we get into the extreme end of identifying rarities and even subspecies of rarities, things often get very nitty-gritty on the fine details, and twitchers are on the front line, examining primary projections, looking at tertial fringes, or even collecting poop for DNA samples!

Bird for long enough in your local area, and you'll see a twitch. Just wait for that one big rarity to turn up and watch as your quiet little field becomes a scrum.

Patcher - This is where the cool kids are nowadays. A patcher combines the twitcher's expertise and dedication with an unshakable loyalty to a particular 'patch'. This is usually a specific reserve, but might be a gravel pit, a stretch of coast or even a suburban park.

The patcher knows everything about their patch. They know what birds breed there and in what numbers. They know within a couple of days when the first Willow Warbler will appear. They know that a Coot is an extremely rare bird here and get almost as excited at seeing one as they would if a Lammergeier flew over. They know that if the wind has been blowing strong NE all night, before changing to a SW at dawn, that it is time to get the scope out.

Most impressive of all, they find rarities. Of course they do. If you look at one place long enough and hard enough, you will eventually find something interesting. Then they might cause a twitch!

You should definitely see if you can find a patcher on your, errr, patch, as they will quickly decant more information into your little head than 10,000 pages of this waffle could ever hope to.

Sea Watcher - A strange and rugged breed! Sea watchers are able to endure super-human levels of discomfort, as they hunch under umbrellas in gale force winds on soggy headlands for hours on end. Yep, sea watching isn't everyone's cup of tea.

Sea watchers need scopes. Interesting sea birds like skuas and shearwaters don't like the land – they actively avoid it in fact, so even when strong winds and extreme weather push the birds close in to shore, they tend to keep their distance. What a sea watcher calls a 'good view' of a bird is what a normal birder would call a 'distant view', as this lazy illustration demonstrates-

SHEARWATERS

Sea watchers don't need to march around looking for birds – quite the opposite! They sit still for a very long time and wait for the birds to come to them - well, zip past them at least. Sea watchers like to keep accurate counts of passing birds.

Maybe more than any other birding, though, there is a kind of strange camaraderie in sea watching. The very futility and ridiculousness of it brings out a kind of war-time spirit in people as they sit in dreadful conditions for hours on end, sometimes for very scant reward.

What is the allure? Well, the stormy sea has its own beauty of course, but more than that, I think it is the mystery! Petrels, shearwaters and skuas are strange, alien, birds and carry an aura of intrigue with them. There is also the thought that *anything* can happen out there in the vast sunken mysteries of the deep. Some completely insane lost tropical rarity might fly past, or you may see a whale, a shipwreck, or a sea-serpent!

Ornithologist - An ornithologist is a bird scientist. They might be birders, too, but their motivation is completely different. In my experience, birders have an almost spiritual connection with their hobby – an appreciation for the beauty and mystery of it all. An ornithologist, on the other hand, is probably more interest in dissecting birds or tracking them than admiring them.

Calling a birder an ornithologist is a bit like calling a gardener a botanist.

Photographer - Increasingly, birding and photography are becoming intertwined. Most serious birders nowadays will carry a camera with them, as it helps keep a record of what they have seen, and also lets them share their sighting visually online. There is also the importance of a 'record shot' where a photograph proves the existence of a rarity that otherwise might have been viewed with suspicion. There are also plenty of instances of photos leading to identification of birds which would otherwise have slipped through the net. A bird only seen for a fleeting instance and 'snapped' can be identified at leisure, saving that Dusky Warbler the ignominy of being recorded as a 'Probable Chiffchaff'.

But some people are bird photographers through and through. Their aim isn't to observe or tick a bird - it is to capture the perfect image that will be the envy of all their photographer friends. Maybe they'll win a competition, or get it printed in one of the birding magazines.

Increasingly, there seems to be a largely unnecessary tension between birders and 'toggers (as they are disparagingly called). And sometimes you can see why – irresponsible photographers get too close to birds, they flush them out with recordings, they climb over fences into restricted reserves. There is also the idea that 'they aren't proper birders' as evidenced by 'no bins', and are simply benefitting from all the hard work the patchers did finding that bird in the first place.

Of course, this is a bit silly. There are goodies and baddies on both 'sides' – there are awful birders and awful photographers, and lovely birders and lovely photographers.

Attributes of a good birder

If I were to design the ultimate birder - a kind of birding terminator sent from the future to bird the hell out of the present, what attributes would it have? What traits should you be trying to cultivate to get the most out of your hobby? Here are my suggestions.

Physical attributes - The perfect birder would have good eyesight and hearing, a steady hand, and hardiness.

Birding is largely about looking at things through binoculars, so a sharp eye and a steady hand on the bins is really helpful. An ear for bird calls is also useful. Sadly, as we get older, our senses begin to dull – I'm often told that older birders 'lose' the thin call of the Goldcrest as their hearing tunes out the higher frequencies. If your hearing or eyesight are a bit dodgy, though, don't panic, you can still make a great birder.

Probably more important is endurance. Not necessarily having the ability to trek large distances or scramble up mountains (although this would be useful), but just the ability to endure the elements. Birding is at its best in autumn and spring when the weather is unpredictable and often miserable. Be prepared to be stuck in one uncomfortable place for a long time.

Mental attributes - Patience, integrity, and curiosity.

Patience is definitely my biggest weakness. Really good birders have the patience of a lump of granite - able to just wait and wait with nothing happening until their reward materializes in front of them. I'm far too hyperactive and end up stomping all over the place. Never underestimate the value of staying still.

Integrity. Does that Black Swan that escaped from the zoo down the road really count as birding? Can you put it on your list? That young Kittiwake could have been a Sabine's Gull, right? That distant dot just dropped into the trees where the Hen Harrier had been seen yesterday, so that was probably what it was. Don't fool yourself. If you start down this naïve path your sightings will become pretty hollow and worthless, and, worse still, other birders will view you with suspicion.

Curiosity is definitely the big one. It is what drives the birder to seek new birds and new experiences. It is an open-minded thirst for knowledge that means they get better and better at what they do. A curious birder will look up the sorts of bird they might expect to see that day, and familiarise themselves with their features and calls. A curious birder will keep an eye on the bird news to see what's about and where. A curious birder will ask for help from older, wiser birders – "So, how did you tell that was a Water Pipit and not a Rock Pipit?" A curious birder takes notes on what they've seen so that they learn and remember. A curious birder learns about how the weather, season and habitat affect the bird life around them.

If you're reading this, then you're well on your way to being a curious birder.

Birding Jargon

As soon as you start hanging out with other birders, you will realise that they have a lot of slang terms and no intention of explaining them. You might pick up a few through words context, or by surreptitiously googling them, or even by risking ridicule and actually asking them what on earth they are talking about. I'll save you some bother now by including a little glossary of terms that seem to be in popular parlance today.

Tick – A bird you haven't seen before, and therefore get to 'tick' off your list.

Vagrant – A very lost bird well outside of its natural range. These are rare and exciting birds to see!

Dross – A boring or common bird. A birder might have to sift through a lot of dross in the hope of seeing something more interesting.

Mega – a really exciting find! The bird news may even come out as MEGA!!! With a photo of some unusual Sibe or Yankee. If a 'mega' appears on your patch, go and see it before the twitchers turn up! Actually – I'm joking – they'll already be there somehow.

Sibe – A Siberian species. This is usually reserved for lost little birds that appear in the autumn.

Yankee – An American species. These are really lost. As far as I'm aware, no birds have an active migration route from America to Europe (maybe a few geese pop over from Canada, or a few seabirds loop across the Atlantic and back). A Yankee wader will often pull in the twitchers.

Plastic – An escaped bird or bird of dubious origin. It is 'plastic' – not real, and therefore can't be ticked. Of course, this can lead to all sorts of fun debate if a bird can't conclusively be designated wild or escaped. Some 'plastic' birds can be quite fantastic, but there is always the feeling of 'cheating' and that it is somehow impure to get excited about them. Use your common sense and your gut – if a pelican has clearly just waddled out of the zoo down the road, then do you feel great about going to see it?

Assisted Migration – A bird that has got here on a boat. Yep, really! If an American bird hops on a cruise across the Atlantic, then pops off for a snack on a British harbourside, does it count? I'll let you decide.

LBJ – Little Brown Job. Once you've been birding for a while, you'll notice that there are quite a lot of small brown birds that are hard to distinguish from one another. These are LBJs and are usually Linnets.

Juv/Juvvy – Juvenile. A young bird which often looks distinctly different from the adult. Think of gulls and how the younger ones are a dirty, mottled brown colour compared to the pristine white and grey adults.

Leucistic, Melanistic, Aberrant – You've just seen something really weird in your garden! It looked like a black bird, but was a washed-out ghostly white colour. It must be something rare! After an hour of trawling through the *Collins Guide*, you are none the wiser. Weirdly coloured common birds are commoner than rare birds, and you should never discount this possibility when identifying something unusual. You have just seen a leucistic Blackbird.

A leucistic bird is one that has a mutation making it much paler than normal (think part way to being an albino), whereas a melanistic one is darker. All irregular features like this fall under the umbrella of 'aberrant' – abnormal. Don't let the lack of rarity detract from how cool looking some of these birds are!

Sp. – Yep, pronounced like the end of the word 'crisp'. 'Sp.' is short for species and usually used when birders have seen a bird well enough to place it in a family, but not specific species. For example, fast-flying Guillemots and Razorbills scooting past at a distance are practically indistinguishable, so might be recorded as 'auk sp.' Once, I asked a local birder if he was looking at anything interesting and he replied "Bird sp." Thanks!

Showing Well/Obliging/Confiding – The go-to terms for birders describing a bird that has decided to play ball and perform in front of them.

Skulking/Elusive – The go-to terms for birders describing a bird that has decided not to play ball and hide in a bramble thicket all day.

Putative – The go-to term for a bird that is refusing to be positively identified. If you hear "Putative Caspian Gull," that's just a fancy way of saying "It might be a Caspian Gull."

On territory – a bird seemingly singing and scoping out a place to nest. This can be significant if a bird that usually just 'passes through' your county is planning to start breeding there. It's probably worth noting here that some secrecy can arise around breeding birds –and with good reason! A rare or scarce bird breeding may still attract egg collectors (although this is, thankfully, an increasingly small problem), breeding raptors are still persecuted (either because their eggs could be used for falconry, or because people are protecting vested interest like their grouse), and, of course, some daft birders and toggers might just get too close to the nest and ruin the breeding attempt. Be careful about revealing the breeding sites of birds that aren't dirt common!

Over/ Vismig – Seen flying overhead. At migration time, some really keen eyed (and eared) birders are adept at identifying little black specks as they bounce past overhead. This vismig (visual migration) is often recorded as 'over'. For example – "13 Chaffinch and 1 Hawfinch over." This is actually quite a useful phrase to distinguish them from birds that were actually present 'on patch'.

Jizz – An unfortunate and etymologically mysterious term which is actually quite an important part of birding. Identifying a bird by its jizz means identifying it by 'gut feel' or intuition. Once you get really familiar with a species, you can sometimes identify it just from a flicker in the corner of your eye – something about the size/shape/movement/behavior which just instantly ticks the box – "Oh, that was a Sparrowhawk that I just saw almost subliminally!" Humans are extraordinary pattern recognition machines, so it is perhaps unsurprising that this skill develops. Identifying birds on jizz is an important skill among birders and one you'll begin to develop with practice.

Jam – From 'being jammy', meaning lucky. If you jam onto a rare bird, the implication is that you weren't expecting it or looking for it very hard – maybe the Little Bunting that had been evading everyone all week just popped out in front of your car the second you parked up.

Gripped – The gut wrenching feeling of jealousy that someone is seeing a bird you really want to see but can't because you are stuck at work, or slept in too late. "What? A Honey Buzzard just flew over my patch while I was in the cinema?" Gripped!

Bling – A ringed bird. Birds are ringed in so that ornithologists can better track their movements and migration patterns. Although it seems disruptive (catching a bird in a net and clipping a metal or plastic ring to its leg), the birds aren't harmed, and it can give us important information on the routes birds take and where they breed, allowing us to improve conservation efforts.

With small birds, rings are almost impossible to read, so this invariably means they will need to be retrapped if their number is to be read. But with larger, long-legged birds like gulls and waders, more visible rings can be used – either unique colour coded plastic rings, or rings with large number/letter codes on them. This means that a birder with a good scope or a camera with a powerful zoom can read and submit the sighting and help in the research! This is an increasingly important part of birding and it's nice to know you are helping with the conservation effort.

BOC – Back of Camera. The curious practice of taking a photo of a photo so you can get it up online quicker. This is a grainy phone camera photo of the screen on the back of a DSLR. "Ooh - look what a good photo I will be able to show you later!"

Record Shot – Something birders and photographers will label an image with to make it clear that they aren't professing to have captured an aesthetically or artistically valuable photo - it is simply proof that they saw the bird. Maybe it shows some important ID feature like the pattern on the bird's tail as it blurrily flies away. Look out for really good photos labeled as 'record shots' – a kind of ridiculous humblebrag made by photographers.

Suppression/ suppressing b**rd** – Nothing makes birders angrier than 'suppression' – when someone keeps the presence of a rare bird secret. It is worth noting that this is rarely done maliciously (although I'm sure there are instances where someone has kept a bird to themselves), but more often it is 'suppressed' due to it being in some nervous old lady's garden who would probably have a heart attack if she opened her curtains to see three ranks of beardy men with telescopes staring towards her.

String/Stringy – Unreliable information. A strange phenomenon that you will begin to notice once you start keeping your eye on the bird news – occasionally a surprising or unrealistic report turns up. Now, sometimes these turn out to be true (as we've established, birds can turn up anywhere), sometimes they are the result of genuine mistakes or over-exuberance (Jays being called Hoopoes), and sometimes, just sometimes, they are the result of malice or delusion. However the 'stringy' information appears, learn to recognize it as 'string' and don't get tricked into frantically cycling to your local park to see the Golden Oriole that is a Goldfinch. Sadly, you might find some repeat offenders –'stringers'- on this front. Just ignore them and hope that a 'boy who cried wolf' moment doesn't occur.

Slang for species

On top of these phrases there are a vast number of abbreviations and short names for bird species themselves. In real life, I'm an English teacher, so I probably find the etymology of these more interesting than most! I've included some of the more common and impenetrable ones below, but depending on where you are in the country, you will likely find some ones I've never heard of.

First of all, there are the acronyms and initialisms. These are pretty straightforward and usually reserved for birds with tediously long names. Therefore, Great Northern Divers become GNDs, Long-Eared Owls become LEOs and Great Black-Backed Gulls become GBBGs.

There is actually an official list of initialisms - the BTO (British Trust for Ornithology) 'species codes', which are supposedly used for submitting records. However, like Esperanto, although well-meaning, I've never actually heard of anyone using them. This is probably because of confounding allocations like BJ for Black Tern and AF for Little Tern.

Then there are the abbreviations, employed for a similar reason as the acronyms. Great-Spotted Woodpeckers, becomes Greatspots, Sparrowhawks become Sprawks, Black-Tailed Godwits are Blackwits, while Bar-Tailed Godwits are Barwits. Some of these are quite nice. I like Meadow Pipits better as Mipits, Storm Petrels better as Stormies, and Tufted Ducks better as Tufties. Though I'm not so sure about Grasshopper Warblers becoming Groppers.

There are too many of these to go through here, but at least you can use a bit of common sense to work them out.

More impenetrable, are the Latin and scientific names that get bandied about. I am sure that this is usually done to affect some air of authority and expertise. They are also good ways of covering for not being able to make an exact ID, so a bird that might have been a Sparrowhawk or a Goshawk becomes accipter sp. A little leaf warbler of indecipherable heritage becomes a phyllosc. sp. Were those House Martins or Swallows? Well, either way they were certainly hirundines. Some diving ducks that might have been Tufties or Scaups? No problem - aythaya sp.

Then there are the really fun names - archaic or local dialect names for birds that just seemed to stick. Great Skuas are almost always referred to as Bonxies from some old Scottish dialect. The Black Guillemot is rather wonderfully a Tystie, A Little Grebe a Dabchick, A Lapwing a Peewit, and a Green Woodpecker a Yaffle.

Depending on what part of the country you're from, a House Sparrow might be a Spuggy or a Spadger. And the poor little Hedge Sparrow? Well he's actually a Hedge Accentor, but more frequently called a Dunnock.

Bits of Birds

And another place where birders like to show off their vocabulary is in describing bird parts. This can actually be fairly useful, but I can't help wondering why they aren't more logical and less pretentious. Here's a quick rundown of oft-bandied-about bits of bird anatomy. You'll find a nice diagram of these bits inside most bird guides.

Supercillium – Eyebrow. Lots of birds have a distinctive stripe over the eye that is a key ID feature. I think 'brow' would have been fine.

Lores – The bit between the eye and the beak. No idea why this bit needs a name. The backs of my knees don't even have a name, so why does this?

Mandible – It's a beak mate.

Gonys – The angle of a beak, specifically on a gull. You know that red dot on a Herring Gull's beak? That has a name – the Gonys Spot.

Crown – The top of the head – at least this makes sense.

Nape - The back of the head/neck sort of area.

Mantle – A bit further down again. If a bird was getting a massage it would be focused on the nape and mantle.

Rump – Importantly, this is the bit on top of the bird, just above the tail. Loads of birds display bright white rumps which are useful ID features - Bullfinches, Hen Harriers, Jays, Storm Petrels, House Martins, Curlew Sandpipers and, of course White-Rumped Sandpipers. The name Wheatear actually derives from 'White Arse'. In fact, so many birds have a distinctive white rump it's a wonder it's a useful ID feature at all.

Vent – The actual bum bit. Birds have a 'cloaca' which is a kind of multi-purpose defecating/reproducing port, and this is thankfully concealed by the vent.

Primaries, Secondaries, Tertials – Primaries are the outermost wing feathers (the finger tips), then moving along the wing back towards the bird you will find the Secondaries and Tertials. Really nerdy birders even start numbering these feathers for complex ID gymnastics – P10 is the tenth primary feather from the end of the wing.

Primary Projection – How far the wing tips 'stick out' from the back of the bird. Actually more useful than it sounds when attempting to ID certain birds.

Coverts – 'Covering' feathers that overlap from the bird's shoulder down its wing to its primaries/secondaries/tertials. There are also tail coverts.

Alula – a little feather on the front edge of the wing that gets its own name for some reason. I found a Jay's bright blue alula feather when I was a kid and my dad got it framed.

Mirror – the pattern at the tips of a gull's wing.

Keeping Lists

One of the key things associated with birding is keeping lists.

Adding a new bird to a list is a good feeling. There is a sense of achievement in having found something new, and, as your list gets longer, the distance between new ticks also gets longer, so there is never a diminishing effect on the joy. If anything, it gets better and better. The idea of getting a new bird on your list might get you out of the house when otherwise you would have wasted the day in front of *YouTube*. And maybe when you haul yourself out of bed to go and see that Long-Billed Dowitcher, you end up having a super day seeing lots of other interesting stuff.

But is this endorphin hit taking away from the purity of simply enjoying nature and observing it?

I think the best advice I can give about keeping lists is balance. If you are enjoying the birding as well as getting the bonus of adding a bird to the list, then everything is in balance and you are getting double pleasure. However, if the list becomes the motive for going out rather than the result, then you are straying towards the dark side.

I keep my lists on my computer – just a word document with a number down the left hand side, the name of the bird, the date, and maybe a note of the location. If I want to remember more thoroughly, I can cross-reference the date with one of my old note books.

Anyhow, there's no harm in starting some lists and seeing how it works out for you. Here are some list suggestions.

Life list – This is the big one - the list of every single species of bird you have seen anywhere, anytime. The first bird on the list will be a Wood Pigeon or a House Sparrow, or whatever you see out your window when you first pick up the pen and paper, and the last bird will be that Kakapo you saw last year on your trip to New Zealand.

UK list – This is the one that means most to me, personally. I'm not a big traveler, and when I do go abroad I'm not dedicating the whole time to birding, so my life list is essentially the UK list with a few extras. The satisfaction of a UK list is that it gets increasingly hard to add to. As the ticks get further apart, the sense of achievement and pleasure associated with it increases exponentially. Some birders (well, twitchers really) have UK lists of over 400 birds! Last I checked, I think the record was near 600.

County list – Or maybe some other smaller division of area. All the way down to a...

Patch list – Probably the most rewarding list to keep. Set some firm rules with yourself as to the boundaries of your 'patch' - decide whether birds that are seen from the patch but not actually in it count (I suggest yes), and whether birds flying over the patch but not actually landing in it count (I suggest definitely).

This kind of list helps you get really familiar with a particular place, its rhythms, and its idiosyncrasies. It's also quite fun to get the same endorphin rush you would get from a mega tick on your UK list just by seeing a Yellowhammer or some such on your patch.

Patch lists probably contain more 'value' as conservation information than other lists, too. There will be a way to submit your data to a local birding group and help them get an idea of the lay of the land. Oh, hang on, there is an even smaller list...

Garden list – Why not! If you're lucky enough to have a garden, or at least a window with some sort of view, then you can keep a list of the birds that land in, pass over, or zip past your house.

Year list – This is the dangerous one, I find. The list begins at 1 second past midnight on January the 1st and ends on the stroke of midnight the following December 31st. This kind of list allows you to compare one year to another in terms of species seen and, perhaps more importantly, species missing.

This can be a fun competition with yourself to see if you can bag more birds than you did the year before. But this little game of topping your previous score can be a gateway drug to twitching – you have been warned! Some years I'll keep a year list, but if I find myself getting too caught up in it, I have a year off and just enjoy the birding without the list pressure.

Naturally, you can have a UK year list, a world year list, a patch year list and a garden year list, too.

Day list – This one's a bit silly when you think about it, but can be quite fun. Actually, you'll already be making one of these, of sorts, if you have your notebook with you in the field. Trying to see one hundred different species in a day is a real challenge and will require you to travel through different habitats and take a packed lunch. I've had some good days birding where a friend and I have tried to hit certain targets - '50 before breakfast' is quite fun. Again, though, you are inviting the danger of the list becoming more than the experience. Just watch yourself.

Holiday list – If you are lucky enough to get away somewhere, why not keep a holiday list? This can be a nice addition to your break, but remember that your family probably wants to spend some time with you, too.

Dream List – Bird long enough and you'll start seeing birds in your sleep. Bee-Eaters have made it onto my dream list before my UK list, sadly.

The bottom line with lists is that it should be fun. Like gambling, if it stops being fun and becomes a chore or source of anxiety, then let it go.

Identification

The crux of good birding. ID - confidently separating one species from another so you can add it to your list, or simply appreciate the beauty in variety provided by evolution.

As I've said, this isn't an ID guide – you'll need your *Collins* for that – but I can certainly give you a few tips here to help you become better at identification and therefore a better birder.

Research! - Before you even go birding, have a flip through the *Collins* and look up some of the species you are expecting or hoping to see. It is much easier to ID a bird when you know what it is you're looking for.

For example, you've heard that there is a Wood Sandpiper at a local reserve – heading out with no knowledge, you run the risk of missing it completely, or, worse still, seeing a Green Sandpiper (which are common in this hypothetical reserve) and making an ID blunder. So you look it up before you head out - now you know you should be looking at the edge of muddy pools for a bird smaller than a Redshank that likes to wade quite deep into the water looking for food. Already, you're not wasting time looking in trees or focusing on big birds like Grey Herons. You've also read that the Wood Sandpiper has a really strong supercillium (birder for eyebrow stripe, remember), so can discount all those Green Sandpipers with hardly any brow going on. Maybe you've even listened to its call by searching the internet.

Go out armed with knowledge like this and you will greatly increase your chances of success.

Of course, this won't help you if a bolt from the blue turns up and you see something completely unexpected!

Comparison species - The sandpiper scenario above is an excellent example of this. Basically, you want to get good at common birds - spend time getting to know your Herring Gulls, Dunnocks and Dunlins, and the more unusual species will 'pop out' at you. It's much easier for your brain to build a schema based on comparison than thinking of things in isolation.

For example, Chaffinches (very common) and Bramblings (a little rarer and more interesting) are roughly the same size and colour, and hang out together in the same habitat – often in the same flock. If you weren't looking for one, then you could easily sift through a load of Chaffinches and miss a Brambling. But if you went out with the knowledge that there are Bramblings about, and you had looked up the fact that they have a distinctive bright white line from the base of their tail running up their back (you did your research!), then life becomes much easier. You are scanning the flock of Chaffinches looking for a flash of white on a rump, and hey presto! Brambling. You will then notice all sorts of other little differences and begin to build a stronger set of ID rules for the future.

Size, shape and movement - Think of identification as pruning an enormous tree. This tree represents all the species of birds in the world – this thick branch houses all the birds of prey, with a smaller bough forking off for the falcons, one for the hawks, one for the vultures, etc. Then smaller and smaller sticks branching off these until you end up with little twigs on which sit the individual species. ID, then, is snipping away the branches until you are left with one twig and a positive identification. The quickest way to get down to a manageable shrub is by observing the bird's size, shape and movement.

Mostly, people starting out into identification get pretty hooked on the colours of a bird, but this is actually far less important than these other impressions, especially as colours can be really deceptive at a distance or in different light conditions.

Use your knowledge of commoner comparison species to assess the size of the bird. Is it a dinky thing like a House Sparrow, or even smaller? Is it a middle sized thing like a Blackbird? Is it a chunky monkey like a Wood Pigeon? Or is it something huge like a Herring Gull? Immediately, you are pruning down the possibilities. Some birds are really distinctively sized – A Starling, for instance is an odd size somewhere between a House

Sparrow and a Blackbird which seems to be inhabited by very few species.

Equally important is shape. Obviously, you will see the shape differences between a raptor, a wader and a finch, but shape can be important in separating more subtle differences. Let's use an example of Crows and Ravens – colour wouldn't help you at all. Size might, but without any point of reference how can you be sure that isn't an obese Crow or an anorexic Raven? Well, Ravens have chunky, heavy heads with thick bills, and their tail is long and vaguely diamond shaped which is distinctive in flight. The whole shape is different, with a Raven being more like a big 'flying cross'.

And movement. This seems tricky, as your bird guide can't illustrate this as well as it can colour, size and shape, but it becomes one of the most important and instinctive ID techniques you will develop. Some birds have really distinctive flight patterns or habits that really leap out at you. For example, the Sparrowhawk has a really distinctive flight pattern – *flapflapflap gliiiide, flapflapflap gliiiide.* In combination with the shape (short, rounded wings and a long, square-ended tail) and size (skinny pigeon) it is unmistakable, even when spiraling high up silhouetted against a summer sky.

Sounds - This probably deserves an entire chapter – no – an entire book to itself, and is the most underrated and ignored thing for beginning birders. Knowing birdsongs and calls will multiply your enjoyment and success in birding by a magnitude. Think about it – you are walking through a woodland, or area of scrub, or simply along a hedgerow. How many birds can you hear as opposed to see at any given time?

Straight away, the sound directs you to where you should be looking, so already has a benefit.

But more than that, it can also inform you where to look. In a world where every little bird made exactly the same noise, you would be forced to inspect every little *'peep'* not knowing if you would end up looking at a Wren or a Turkey Vulture. With a little knowledge, knowing the calls of the comparison birds will allow you to ignore the commoner ones and hone in on the sound of something unusual. This is the same trick you used with visual identification – you learn the common birds' calls so that the rare ones 'jump out' at you. You don't need to learn everything!

And just as well, because a single species of bird will often have a large repertoire of sounds. They may have a song, an alarm call, a flight call, and often a range of contact calls, too. And some birds make other noises, as well – Wood Pigeons leap out of trees with a great kerfuffle, woodpeckers drum, Nightjars clap their wings together, Blackbirds rustle as they flip dry leaves over on the floor.

Some birds, like Starlings, confound matters further by copying the sounds of other birds. And some birds, like Great Tits, have an incredibly irritating range of little noises to discombobulate the novice observer. But, with practice, you will realize that even in these confusing scenarios, different species have a particular timbre – just like you would be able to tell the difference between a trumpet and a saxophone regardless of what tune they were playing.

As well as helping you spot birds and find rarities, bird calls will actually help you with identification. Some species, in fact, really require you to hear their call before you can safely ID them, so similar are their appearance. The classic example here is the Marsh Tit and Willow Tit which are almost inseparable without hearing the Willow Tit's harsh little wheeze.

Also, bird calls can tell you a lot about what's going on. If you hear a sudden racket among the local gulls or crows, then get your eyes skywards! There is probably a passing raptor that they are escorting out of town. A similar brouhaha in the woods could lead you to a roosting owl as the daytime birds dish out some revenge on their night time predator.

So endeavour to learn calls and songs. The problem is that even your wonderful *Collins* guide won't help you here – sure, it has phonetic descriptions of bird calls, but it can be hard to imagine these from the print. Instead, you're going to have to observe (audserve?) common singing or calling birds and mentally attach the sound to the bird. A great book on this subject is *Birdwatching with your Eyes Closed* by Simon Barnes which was an invaluable and accessible introduction to this subject for me. Another great resource is the internet – a website called *Xeno Canto* is full of free recordings of birds taken from all over the world, and can be really useful to try and match up something you've heard with its perpetrator.

Can you 'tick' a bird off your list if you only hear it? I'll leave you to decide!

Time and place -If you read the section on location and time of year, you're already a bit of an expert on this, and this'll help you narrow things down. Some birds simply cannot be that species because they are in completely the wrong habitat, or at completely the wrong time of year.

For example, a small nondescript female duck on a pool in winter is likely a Teal, but very unlikely to be a Garganey which, although pretty damn similar, is (unusually for a duck) a summer visitor. That female Redstart you saw on the roof of your shed last November? That was a Black Redstart, not only because all the Redstarts would have been in Africa by then, but because they are exclusively into trees, where Black Redstarts, for some reason, like guttering.

This rule of time and place is really useful until it isn't. Remember, that birds can turn up anywhere, and seeing a Swallow on Christmas Day, or a Manx Shearwater in a shrubbery is entirely within the realms of possibility.

Notes, sketches and photos - This is a tediously old-school thing to suggest, but taking detailed notes, and if you've got some drawing ability, sketching birds, is one of the best routes to getting good at ID. The best birders I've met are bird artists. Why? Well, because they are looking really closely at a bird to capture its likeness – much closer than if they were just enjoying looking at it, and certainly much closer than someone taking a photo, who will inevitably be more worried about the focus and ISO and aperture and white balance and blahblahblah. Trying to describe, either in image or words, what you see requires a deeper level of observation and a real connection with the features of a species.

Also, detailed notes and sketches will help you identify something that was a mystery at the time. You might, of course, have your ID guide with you (fine), but by the time you've thumbed through it a few times, whatever you were looking at has likely gone. Unless it's a Spoonbill, in which case, it's still asleep. But then, being rather distinctive, you probably wouldn't need to look up a Spoonbill!

SLEEPY SPOONBILL.

I don't mean to be derisory to photography and photographers, and, indeed, a good photo is going to give you the most rock-solid identification aid you could hope for. I've even seen birders use photos to prove that a rare bird seen in the north of the country is the same as a bird seen in the south a week later, by zooming in and making detailed comparison of the feather patterns. No need to go this far, though – snap away and identify at your leisure if that's your thing!

Ask - Finally, and perhaps most dauntingly, why not ask for help? I would say that the majority of birders will help you willingly with an ID question, but in my experience that isn't entirely true. I think just less than half would be helpful and just over half would be surly, dismissive or patronising. Still, no harm done! Keep asking until you find a nice one and you'll not only get the answers you're after, but probably a useful lesson on how they made their identification. Also you've learnt who to avoid in the future.

Chiffchaff vs Willow Warbler

Let's put your newfound ID skills to the test to solve a classic birding challenge! The Chiffchaff and the Willow Warbler are such similar species that you will sometimes see them recorded as 'Willowchiffs' – someone wasn't sure which they were. A more proud birder might record them as phillosc. sp. But essentially this means the same thing.

Actually, though, these two aren't as hard to tell apart as you might think – there are much trickier species to separate out there for sure. Get this one under your belt and you'll feel really good about yourself and ready to take on whatever ID challenges the birding world throws at you.

Let's set the scene. You are on a scrubby heathland with some young willow trees in April, and a delicate little browny-greeny warbler hops onto a branch in front of you. It's paler underneath than on top and has a paleish stripe above its eye. Otherwise, it's pretty nondescript. Willowchiff. Well, the habitat and time of year aren't going to help you, I'm afraid! Chiffchaffs like willow trees, too, and both species are in the UK at this time. If this were taking place in January, then you could be confident of a Chiffchaff, many of which stay here while the Willow Warblers go to sun themselves in Africa.

What is it your granddad said? Chiffchaffs have black legs and Willow Warblers have pink legs. Great! This should be easy. Oh, if only the bloody thing would stay still long enough that you could see its legs. Blimey, who thought a tiny, fast-moving bird's legs would be so small and hard to see? Also, I'm afraid to say, your grandad wasn't really spot on with this one – you can get Willow Warblers with pretty dark legs. On the whole, yes, Willow Warblers are going to have pale legs and be a little brighter and cleaner looking than Chiffchaffs, but this isn't going to seal the deal.

What was it the experts said? Ah! Primary projection! A Willow Warbler migrates further than a Chiffchaff, so it has longer wings. The primaries are the wingtip feathers, and poke out quite a lot beyond the bird's bum on a perching Willow Warbler, whereas a Chiffchaff's wingtips only just reach beyond their backside. Okay, this is even harder to see than the legs, especially at this angle! Actually, this is quite useful, and when you are really familiar with Chiffs (familiar enough to call them Chiffs, for instance), then a Willow Warbler will suddenly look very sleek and long-winged. But let's say we can't quite get a fix on this.

Oh, now it made a sound! A little *'hweet?'* call. No good. Both Willow Warblers and Chiffchaffs do this! Some people say they can tell the *'**hw**eet?'* of a Willow Warbler and the *'hw**eet**?'* of a Chiffchaff apart, but I don't believe them.

What have we got left? Colour, shape, sound, location and time of year have all been inconclusive. How about movement? Now we're talking.

This particular bird is bumbling rather clumsily about and keeps dipping its tail as if it's losing balance when it lands on a branch. It's a Chiffchaff. Yep. That easy. Willow Warblers are so much more graceful and poised in their movement and aren't always doing that daft tail-bobby thing.

And now it's decided to sing *'chip chap chip chap chap chap chip (brrr brrr)'* yep, the little dunce can't even get his name right. A Willow Warbler would have a lovely trickling little song that starts confident and peters out into embarrassment – *'That Brian from accounts, he's such an odious, oh he's standing right behind me isn't he?'* *'I watched this great documentary on diesel trains and, oh you really don't care do you?'*

Willowchiffs

In reality, identification of Willowchiffs is a bit of a combination of the above. If it sings, then your problem is instantly solved, but otherwise you are working on the impression of the bird and the way it moves. If you have ever known any identical twins then you soon learn to tell them apart, and Willowchiffs are the same. Put simply, the Willow Warbler is the

Chiffchaffs cooler, more elegant twin sister. Sound silly? Well, I challenge you to go and separate a Willow Warbler and a Chiffchaff and see what I mean!

Once you've done that, then you'll be ready for Arctic vs. Common Terns ('Commic Terns') or Black-Tailed vs. Bar-Tailed Godwits. Good luck!

Birding and the Internet

This is such a huge part of modern birding. Generally, I'm a bit of a grump when it comes to social media, but if there's one place it's useful, it's this, and there are a number of reasons why the internet is the modern birder's best friend (after your binoculars, of course).

Twitter – *Twitter*, rather aptly, has become the go-to place to report bird sightings. Don't worry about all the celebrity feuds, political polls and goading trolls – just mute them and follow your local birders. It is concise, instantaneous, can include photos and maps. It's just great. Back in the day, birders used pagers, and I guess this is just the logical evolution of those.

There are also a number of nationwide bird news twitter accounts, the most famous, surely being *@RareBirdAlertUK*. But you will also soon find that many of your local birders have a twitter account which will keep you up to date with what they've seen locally – great if you want to go on a mini-twitch, or simply if you are deciding where to go, or what to research before heading out. Once you've found one local birder, you can find all the rest by seeing who they follow and joining suit. There are even a number of funny birding twitter accounts dedicated solely to birding humour!

Once you've set up your own account, you can start posting your own sightings. More on this later.

Bird Forums – Not only are there huge international forums for discussing birding (*Bird Forum* being the most famous), but as far as I know, every county has its own bird news site. In some cases, a particular reserve might even have its own site. The rise of *Twitter* as a bird news medium has made these a little less popular than they once seemed to be, but they're still great sites to have saved in your favourites.

This is another place where people go to post sightings and pictures of what they've seen, and though a little less instant than twitter, can be a great place to get wind of something interesting. Furthermore, once you have followed the local bird news for a while, you will probably find yourself involved to a degree where you want to join a local birding society.

You might even find help with ID here, if you have seen something unusual and have either photos or descriptions to upload – but make sure that you are posting in the right forum – some sites get grumpy with ID questions cluttering up the news feed.

ID – Although the *Collins Guide* is wonderful, it can't show you sounds and moving images in the way the net can. I've already mentioned *Xeno Canto* as a source of bird calls, but *YouTube* has plenty of great ID videos, too. I must particularly mention the *BTO* ID videos which are great for learning to separate some tricky species.

Maps, Tides and Weather – Again your smartphone comes to the rescue when out and about. Maps will help you find specific off the track locations where birds have been seen, and keeping up to date with tides and weather conditions is essential birding knowledge if you want any success.

Blogs – Finally, there are the blogs – little diaries added by birders on niche little subjects. Here you will find detail on tricky ID's, mad theories about migration, and really in depth little tidbits of local bird news. Again, you will need to seek out the ones that are relevant to you, but it's all good stuff.

Posting Your Findings

Whether on *Twitter* or a local Bird Forum, there is going to come the point when you want to share your findings via the internet. In fact, it would be criminal not to! Don't end up being a suppressor just out of shyness, especially if you find something interesting.

But there are a few pitfalls here to be avoided, so here's some friendly advice!

Make sure you're sure - Especially when posting something rare or unusual. No one wants the embarrassment of starting a panic amongst the twitchers. Imagine that! You say you've seen a Lesser Yellow-Legs on a local scrape, and birders from miles around pack up what they are doing to drive there and look at a Greenshank. Ouch!

If you aren't sure, then the best thing to do is get some confirmation from a more experienced birder – hopefully you've met a nice one by now - get a direct message to them by text or twitter and see if they can help before you 'go public'.

Keep it concise - Even if you're the most wonderfullest wordsmith since the Bard himself, people don't want to trawl through the epic novel of your day out, just to hear that you saw a Jack Snipe. Of course, a little description is fine, but a nice trick is to highlight the species names in **bold**, so that people less appreciative of your prose can hone in on the gist of your writing.

Think about what people actually want to know - This might seem a little harsh, and even a little against the spirit of this guide, but I'm always mystified slightly by people posting that they saw 3 Blue Tits and a Chaffinch in their garden. The likelihood is that most people have these birds in their garden – it's not news.

Personally, I don't really get angry about this (though some birders do), but I think it's worth asking yourself if your news is news before you post.

Don't give away sensitive information - Sadly, some birds – particularly birds of prey – are persecuted, either by egg collectors or gamekeepers (or over-zealous photographers!), so it's important to keep breeding locations secret. Sure, seeing a Goshawk is literally one of the most exciting things that can happen to you birding, but if you need to tell everyone, make sure you keep the location vague. As with point one, if you aren't sure, get some help from a trustworthy local birder before posting.

Taking other people Birding

May seem like a good idea, but remember that not everyone is quite as mad as you. The important thing about taking people birding is making sure they know what to expect and to 'manage their expectations'.

I'm not talking about birding with other birders – that's a different thing. More eyes means less chance of missing something. I'm talking about birding with laymen.

It's natural, when getting excited about a new hobby that you will want to share it with people – "See what you've been missing! Isn't this great!" But not everyone really cares about the difference between a Willow Warbler and a Chiffchaff, and even fewer want to stomp around a muddy field getting cold for hours on end. So as well as managing their expectations, you need to manage yours, too. Don't push it as far as you would normally, and maybe sweeten the deal with a trip to the pub afterwards for lunch, even if it does mean you miss seeing that Grey Phalarope.

And bear in mind the possibility of your friends being bird magnets or bird repulsers. This might be a lot to do with how loud, clumsy and talkative they are – someone who bellows and crashes about in the undergrowth is going to scare birds off, whereas someone a little more reserved might let you actually listen out for bird calls. But there also seems to be an element of lucky and unlucky people (as silly as that sounds) – I have a friend who dresses entirely in bold black and white, doesn't carry binoculars, smokes like a chimney and has one of the loudest voices known to man, but when he comes along for a stroll, Ospreys soar overhead, skuas skim the beach and warblers fall out of the sky. He's always welcome.

Anyway, there's a lot of reward to be had in taking a birding gentile out if you get it right. Just look at them light up when they see a Goldfinch or some other common, but handsome bird through a good pair of binoculars for the first time. It might even, after a few years, help you reconnect with how handsome Goldfinches are.

Other Animals

When you're out looking for birds, immersed in the environment and sneaking about, you will, inevitably end up seeing other creatures, too, and, if you're anything like me, getting fascinated by what you see. Indeed, birding is a bit of a gateway drug.

Butterflies, moths and dragonflies - Will probably be the first things that grab your attention outside of birds – after all they fly about, too. And they conveniently seem to be most active when the birding is at its worst. Butterflies, in particular, are pretty easy for a birder – there are only a few species and they are generally pretty easy to identify. It won't be long before you're keeping a list of them, too. Moths, though, are the real prize – after all, butterflies are just moth tarts. You might even find yourself investing in (or building!) a moth trap to explore the variety of species that go about their business while you dream.

Reptiles and Amphibians – Are also pretty damn interesting. As a birder, you'll be out early in the morning, just when the snakes and lizards are trying to get their body temperature up by lying around in the middle of the road. There's nothing quite like seeing an Adder coiled in your path on a cool early summer morning.

Mammals – Mammaling isn't a word for a reason - it is a bit more difficult. They tend to be very secretive, but your encounters, when you do have them are guaranteed to be surprising and sudden, whether it is a Stoat scooting across your path, a Fallow Deer foal disturbed by your presence, or a Hare, well, haring away across a field.

Bats are a different thing again, and an obvious progression for aerophile observers. And if you want to ID them, you'll need a bat detector - a clever little device for identifying species of bats by the frequency of their calls.

But what about the sea mammals! If you are mad enough to be into sea watching, then you will inevitably experience cetaceans such as porpoises and dolphins of several species. To date, I still think my best 'birding' experience was seeing a Humpback Whale breaching out of the sea on my patch. Oh! And don't forget those charming seals, but is it a Grey Seal or a Common?

Fish - And while we're looking out to sea, what about Sharks? Ocean Sunfish? Leaping Tuna? All possible.

And why stop at animals? What about Fungi? Wild flowers? Trees?

Yep, you're going to amass quite a lot of ID guides to satiate your desire to taxonomies everything.

Ten Birds worth Seeing

All birds are worth seeing of course! But I've picked this short list (after much agonizing) to give you a few targets early on in your birding adventure. They aren't super rare, and they aren't all necessarily particularly colourful or extravagant, but they are all spectacular in their own way, and in hunting them down you will explore some of the different aspects of birding. They're all stunners.

Jay - Okay, so this one is colourful! Absurdly so, in fact.

As well as being a rather fetching shade of pink, with that wonderful patch of azure blue on the wing, Jays are full of character. This is because they are actually crows. Remember when I said that size and shape were more useful ID features than colour? Well, when you see your first Jay, imagine it in silhouette – large and chunky, with a thick beak and a hopping gait. Clearly a crow. I always think it strange that a bird from a family famous for being monochrome should be so gaudy.

Jays really like trees - a trait that might make a more eloquent guide describe them as 'arboreal'. They feed almost exclusively on acorns, and, like squirrels, spend a lot of their time collecting them and stashing them away for the winter. In fact, if you see a randomly growing Oak tree a good distance from any others, the chances are that it was planted by a forgetful Jay.

Getting a good look at a Jay is going to require your birding skills of stealth and patience, as they are wary and watchful birds, and your first view will probably be a glimpse of its bright white rump as it dashes away from you through the trees. And as well as that view, you will probably be treated to the Jay's alarm call – a sound so ugly, it feels like it was designed to counterbalance the Jay's visual beauty – a kind of hoarse, piercing 'kraaa!' This is doubly annoying as it serves to scare off all the other birds you might want to see in the area, a habit that causes my grandad to refer to them as 'Policeman of the woods'.

Jays are like a lot of 'unobvious' birds in that once you've seen one, they start popping up everywhere. I think this is because they are actually fairly common – even in parks and gardens – but because they're shy they often go unnoticed. Once you are familiar with their slow, bounding flight (and that raucous call, of course) you will see a Jay almost every day.

Gannet - To see a Gannet, you will need to get to the coast. Ideally somewhere with a good view of a wide, open stretch of sea. Scan the skies with your bins. You won't see a Gannet on the land, and they don't really sit on the sea for long, either.

The first thing you will notice is that Gannets are huge and brilliant white - much cleaner and more majestic than the gulls that will inevitably be flapping around. Their long, pointed wings are jet black at the ends as if dipped in ink. Look at how effortlessly these huge birds soar around over the waves. But watch what happens next!

Gannets fish by diving head first into the sea, often from a great height. Watch as they turn into living darts, fold their wings back and plummet into the waves. And what a splash! If you're lucky, you might even get to see a feeding frenzy where whole legions of Gannets are plunging into the sea assaulting a shoal of fish – one of the most spectacular birding sights. Watch where they hit the water and you might also get a glimpse of porpoises or dolphins attacking the same shoal of fish from below.

Starling - This should be an easy one! These little darlings are common in cities and parks as well as farmland, wetland and moorland. They are what bird guides might call 'ubiquitous'.

However, its ubiquitousness shouldn't distract from its awesomeness. Catch a single Starling singing in the sunlight and look at how the light causes rainbows of purples and greens to shimmer on its initially black-looking feathers like petrol in a puddle - iridescent. And that song! The Starling's song, although distinctive in its own right, is actually a mimicry of other birds it has heard. Listen carefully and you'll probably pick out Swift, Curlew and Magpie among others. They even mimic non-bird sounds and you'll find urban

Starlings doing good impressions of ringing phones and reversing lorries.

Already pretty cool, but the Starling has one more trick up its sleeve. Murmurations. A murmuration is a 'mega flock' of birds which gather together to roost in the winter months – they particularly like to gather in reed beds where they can huddle together in the safety of the stems. And when I mean 'mega flock' I am talking serious numbers – thousands or even tens of thousands. The birds form amazing tight flocks that somehow fly about in coordinated 'clouds' of birds without all crashing into each other. These flocks create all sorts of strange, shifting, beautiful shapes. What you might not expect, though, when seeing your first, murmuration is the sound. If you are lucky enough to be close under the birds as they fly in to roost, the sound of tens of thousands of tiny wings beating at once is quite amazing.

There are numerous excellent places to see this in the UK – there's even a website to help you find your local murmuration! www.*starlingsintheuk.co.uk*. As this is essentially a roosting behavior, you will need to get the time of day right – just before dusk is best, as the birds begin to gather, but you could also aim to see them emerge from their roost at the first light of morning. Don't forget that this is a winter thing, so don't expect to see much murmuration activity in the summer.

As an extra bonus, all this activity is going to attract predators seeking a tasty Starling snack. Murmurations can be great places to see all kinds of birds of prey, from a Sparrowhawk to a…

Peregrine Falcon - Another awesome bird. The Peregrine falcon holds the gold medal for being the fastest animal on the planet – though it does cheat, in my opinion, by setting this record while plummeting headfirst towards the ground, in its iconic 'stoop'.

Now, a Peregrine might take a little more work than a Starling or a Gannet, partly because it is a protected species and as such its nesting places are often kept secret. That said, there are numerous well-documented nesting sites, too – some even have hidden webcams, so you can watch the birds raise their chicks. This is because Peregrines, although naturally cliff nesters, have really taken to nesting on tall buildings like churches or cathedrals. The chances are, your local town has a pair of Peregrines nesting somewhere.

If you intend to find them at their nesting place, then using your ears is going to be your best bet. In late spring through to early summer, they are very noisy – making a shrill, hoarse repetitive cry as they swoop in to feed their babies, who, themselves making an incessant squealing noise. Be careful, though! As Peregrines eat pigeons and other urban 'pests', some places actually have recordings of Peregrines playing on a loop as a way of scaring them off – don't be caught out by this!

Outside of the nesting site, your experience of Peregrines is more likely to be incidental than planned, though they do have some favoured perches – roofs, branches, or ledges, which you may discover if you are paying attention to your patch work.

Your best bet is to keep your eyes on the sky - Look out for a bulky, stocky bird of prey with broad, but pointed wings and a fan shaped tail. They fly with shallow, fast wingbeats in a manner which will become distinctive with familiarity. On breezy days, they like to 'surf' on the wind in order to gain height easily and help them hunt.

And this is the best time to watch these awesome predators. They gain height, and then use their amazing eyesight to pick out a bird flying below them before plunging towards them in a steep dive. Pigeons are amongst their favourites, though waders and ducks are also on the menu, as well as smaller birds. Imagine the skill and timing required to hit a fast-flying pigeon from above with precision! And hit them they do, hammering into them in an explosion of feathers. Violence!

Nightjar - You are going to need to go on a special trip to see one of these, but my goodness, it'll be worth it.

Nightjars arrive in Britain in May and make their way to very specific breeding habitats. They nest on the ground so need areas of undisturbed heather or scrub, but also like forested areas, especially coniferous ones so they have high places to 'sing' from. On top of this, they feed on nocturnal insects like moths, so require open glades or heaths to glide around in pursuit of their prey. You'll need to check your local bird news to find suitable sites near you.

As already mentioned, moths are high on the Nightjar's menu, so, as if you were looking for bats, you will need to be out at dusk to catch sight of them. And when you do? What weird and wonderful birds they are! They are surprisingly hawk-like in shape, with their long slim wings and tail, and they fly in a most bizarre 'slow motion' bouncing manner that, quite frankly, looks like it's been badly CGI'd. Add to this the vivid white flashes on their wings that stand out against the gloaming, and the way they occasionally 'slap' their wings loudly together, and you will appreciate that watching them is a surreal, almost dream-like experience. And I haven't even mentioned the noise they make!

A Nightjar's mating call is called 'churring' - a loud, clockwork whirring rattle. It's straight out of a horror movie! Beautiful, eerie, and one of the best birding moments you can have in this country – I guarantee it!

Great-Crested Grebe - I wanted to put a duck or goose on the list, but I have a bit of a blind spot for waterfowl. I can't help it. I just can't get excited about ducks. So this is a sort of compromise – a grebe.

Grebes are vaguely duck-like water birds which dive under the water to catch small fish and invertebrates. Great-Crested Grebes are probably the most common in this country, and certainly the most elegant.

You can find GCGs on lakes and canals, and, in the winter, even on the sea. But I recommend you go for a spring grebe watch, when they are in their pomp. They should be easy to see, as they happily float around right in the middle of open water. They have very long, slender white necks and a ridiculous sort of ruff and ears combo on their face - like a little lion's mane, perhaps.

Already pretty cool. But if you've got your time of year right, and you have a little bit of luck, you might get to see some of the mating dance. Grebes have an elaborate courtship ritual which is really great to watch. Firstly, you might just notice two Grebes mimicking each others' movements – a little twist of the head this way, then that. Then the fun starts, they collect bits of pond weed, and then carry it towards one another as if delivering a precious present, and end by paddling vertically upwards out of the water, chest to chest, in what is often termed the 'penguin dance'. It's a wonderful thing to see, and not as rare as you'd think.

Swift - Quite probably my favourite bird (don't tell Waxwings). The Swift doesn't actually spend a lot of time in this country – they are among the last migrants to arrive, not appearing until late April, and amongst the earliest to leave, scooting off again in early September. But they really do bless us with their presence in their short stay.

When they do appear, they appear with a scream! The shrill shriek of a Swift is one of the most nostalgic sounds I can think of, taking me straight back to the endless summer holidays of childhood. The way they make this joyful 'Scree! Scree!' as they chase each other across the sky and round the eaves of houses is wonderfully evocative.

Although superficially similar to the hirundines (swallows and martins), Swifts are actually quite distinct both in appearance and behavior. Just look how alien their shape is – a dark scythe that slices its way across the sky. Their strange, crescent moon shaped wings don't bend at the 'elbow' in the way other birds' wings do, giving their dashing flight a strange almost mechanical rigidity.

The reason Swifts don't go in for normal wings is that they don't land. It's pretty cool to think, that if a Swift nests in the eaves of your house, it is literally the only place where it ever touches down, anywhere. Take a moment to imagine them eating in the air (by plucking flies out of the ether), mating in the air, drinking in the air (by skimming low over a pond with their bottom mandible stuck out), and even sleeping in the air, by climbing high before spiraling downwards in a doze. If they could lay eggs in the air, I'm sure they would!

Waxwing - Ah! Waxwings, hello! Did I ever tell you, you are my favourite birds?

These little devils are a bit special, and almost didn't make it onto this list because of difficulty. But other than being absolutely gorgeous, they have another interesting quality that makes them worthy of a beginner's attention.

They're what are called an 'irruptive' species. This means that we aren't actually on their yearly migratory schedule at all – instead, they only turn up here when a particular set of conditions are met. Firstly, they need to have had a good breeding season up in the remote forests of Scandinavia and Siberia, so good, in fact, that when the weather starts to turn. they realize that there won't be enough food to sustain all of them. This sparks a mass migration south and west. So you will be unlikely to see a Waxwing every year, but about every four or five years, you'll get a

'Waxwing winter' where flocks start turning up wherever there are berries.

Yep, they are greedy little blighters, too. They seem to do little except eat red berries (which can make them a bit drunk!) and poop them out again, and they are almost always in groups. Their wonderful combination on naivety (most of them have probably never even seen a human before) and gluttony means that they will turn up in the silliest places. Suburban streets, supermarket carparks and motorway verges seem to be favourites. Get ready for a potential Waxwing winter by staking out sources of red berries nearby, and then check them regularly once the invasion eventually begins! Once those berries are gone, the Waxwings will move on.

Goldcrest - Britain's smallest bird. Goldcrests put me in mind of little mice scurrying around in the foliage of trees. Even their body shape is adorable – like fluffy little pompoms. But don't let their size and appearance fool you, like most little birds, they have a serious 'Napoleon complex', always up for a fight. There's something deeply amusing about the pugnacious little 'Crest raising its crest in an angry frown and having a go at a fellow Goldcrest, a larger tit, or even its own reflection in a window!

And they're tough, too. Many Goldcrests are in this country all year round, but a great number travel here from Scandinavia for the winter. Imagine such a small bird making it across the North Sea in autumn. In the past, people simply refused to believe this, and assumed that they hitched rides on the back of Short-Eared Owls, earning them the rather cool name 'Owl Pilots'!

Goldcrests feed exclusively on insects, and particularly little spiders which they pluck from the underside of leaves, either by hovering in the air, or creeping along a branch. Because of this, you are most likely to find them in evergreen patches of Ivy or Holly in winter.

Like with a lot of little birds, you are more likely to hear them before you see them – that is if you are young enough that your hearing hasn't yet tuned out their very high-pitched call. They communicate in a series of very thin, high 'zeep zeep zeep' sounds. In spring, the remaining Goldcrests will start to sing with the same high, thin tone - a kind of galloping build up of notes ending in a flourish. If you are familiar with the Chaffinch's song, I always think that it sounds like that, but pitch-shifted up!

And the best thing about Goldcrests, is that once you've looked at about a thousand of them, one will turn out to be a Firecrest instead. An absolutely cracking bird that, although superficially similar to a Goldcrest is much brighter, with a striking black and white mask. And once you've seen about a hundred of them, one might just be a Yellow-Browed Warbler.

Dunlin, Redshank, Curlew - In the interest of balance, I thought I'd add a wader to the list. But I appreciate that Waders are all much of a muchness for the beginning birder, so I've lumped three in together. They all have longish legs and longish bills and are various shades of greyish-brown as they wander around distantly in the mud. Sure, they are impressive in large numbers, in much the same way as Starlings are, but individually, they can leave you feeling a little cold.

But they are very instructive! And that's why you should nail down your common waders in your ID schema. Go to your nearest estuary (making sure that it is winter and the tide is right), and sit yourself down in a hide with a nice flask of tea and some biscuits – you're going to learn a lot.

Because waders are all a longish-legged, longish-billed, greyish-brown, you will need to get to grips with size, shape and behavior – something that, I appreciate, I am probably banging on about now. I can almost guarantee that, from your comfy spot in the hide, you'll be able to see all three of these species. Ideally, they'll be awake and feeding, but the chances are they'll be asleep.

The little ones are Dunlin – cute little clockwork toys. They are whitish underneath and grayish on top, and have straightish black bills and legs. Some might have a blackish smudge on their belly which is a remainder from their summer colours. If they fly, you'll notice a distinctive black line down the middle of the tail. This is your benchmark small wader.

Scan along until you find a Redshank. It has bright reddish-orange legs (as its name suggests), but otherwise is also whitish underneath and greyish on top. See if you can get one in the same view as a Dunlin and look at the size difference. Now we're learning something! It's got the same sort of straight looking bill, but is much taller and longer in shape. When these fly, they have a distinctive black and white blocked pattern on the wings. This is your benchmark medium wader.

Now what about that big 'un with the curved bill? That's your benchmark large wader – the Curlew. Curlew's are a sort of mottled, brown pattern all over, and are much bigger than the Redshank. They have a long, elegant neck, and an absolutely absurd bill which is very long, thin and curved downwards. When they fly, they show a big white patch up their lower back from the tail.

Now you can really start birding. Look at your Dunlins, Redshanks and Curlews and start to look for birds that are in between sizes, or have different shapes bills and you will start racking up the species in n time. Between a redshank and a Curlew in size, with a long straight bill? Well, that going to be a Godwit. Like a Redshank in size, but with pale legs and a slightly upturned bill? That's a Greenshank. Like a Redshank but with a shorter bill? Woohoo! That's a Ruff –good bird! What about that one which is between Redshank and Dunlin? That's a Knot. And so on.

Final Thoughts and Birding Badges

So, you're almost ready to go.

I hope that this guide has been useful and that you've picked up a few things that would have taken years to dawn on you otherwise. But, hey, no need to thank me - I'm already glad you bought my little book. If you want to thank me, though, you can find me on *Twitter* with all the other birders, *@earlowlegg* (a cunning anagram of my name).

As a final thought, here's a list of virtual 'birding badges' you could collect as if you were in the Scouts. Think of them as a set of little challenges from me to you to help you on your way.

Patch – Get yourself a patch. This might be a patch that is already 'claimed', but ideally it should be somewhere no one else really bothers with – it could just be the local park, a field, a pond, or a bit of coast. Somewhere really close to home would be ideal so you can nip out and visit a couple of times a week. Start a patch list and a patch year list.

Find a guru – One of your local birders will be the local guru. They will be an absolute expert, a fount of knowledge and really helpful as well. These are the absolute best people to know – get their twitter handle or mobile number so that they can be called on in the case of a birding emergency.

Mini Twitch – Don't charter a plane to the Shetlands, but when a rare or rarish bird is reported within striking distance on your local bird news site, stop what you're doing and go and see it. This will be fun, give you a 'tick' and also allow you to meet all your other local birders for the first time. Look how nervous they are that they might not see it!

First in the hide – Get up *really early* and be the first birder into a bird hide (make sure the tide and time of year is right or this will be a waste of energy). There's a nice quiet satisfaction in being the first one there and you can get the best spot to yourself. Notice how the grizzled birder who arrives 10mins later looks surprised at this Johnny-come-lately who has beaten them to it.

Sketch – Don't be embarrassed at your drawing skills. Like anything, it takes practice. Trying to draw a bird from life will make you look at it in a new way and teach you all sorts of things. Send me your results on *Twitter* – I could do with a laugh.

Do a bird race – Just with yourself, and don't take it too seriously. Set yourself a challenge to do a full day's birding and record as many species as possible. If you want a good score, you'll need to plan carefully – visit various habitats and be in the right place at the right time. End the day by hearing a Tawny Owl hoot and adding it to your list. Eighty is a really respectable score, and a century is excellent.

Read a ring – If you see a ringed bird, try and get a reading. This will be easiest if it's a colour ring on a wader. Do a *Google* search to find out what scheme it belongs to and report it. Now you are actively aiding scientific study and conservation efforts.

Post on the bird news – This doesn't have to be anything super rare, just something locally unusual or something new on your patch. This is a first step to being part of the wider birding community and the birding grapevine. Someone might even find it useful and interesting.

Beat a bogey bird – after a while, you might start to notice you've developed a nemesis. A bird that, although not super rare, seems to evade you at every turn. You always just miss it, or it turns up on your patch while you are on a trip elsewhere. This is the dreaded 'bogey bird'. Mine was a Short-Eared Owl for ages. It feels great when you finally track one down, so go and make the specific effort to do so. Of course, a new bogey bird will soon emerge.

Go somewhere awesome – Treat yourself to a trip somewhere super. This depends on your budget a bit, but there are certain places that really are belting for birding - maybe RSPB Minsmere, the Cairngorms, Shapwick Heath, or if you really want to do something special, Fair Isle or Scilly. Do a little bit of research before you go and make sure you're getting the time of year right. A quick cautionary tale, though:

when I was a kid I used to love snorkeling around Torbay where I grew up. Then I went on holiday in Cyprus and snorkeled in crystal clear water amongst shoals of colourful fish, giant shells and octopuses. When I came home, the thought of chasing a greenish-coloured Shore Crab around a freezing cold cove seemed less appealing – my flippers went unused for many a year.

Take someone birding – Choose the right friend and this'll be great. Or maybe a family member might be a good choice. Introduce them to your wonderful, relaxing hobby and teach them something new. They might even get the bug! If they do, I know a great little book for them…

Printed in Great Britain
by Amazon